Kincaid's Discovery: The Hidden Mysteies of the Grand Canyon

Cassiel E. Nox

Published by Cassiel E. Nox, 2024.

KINCAID'S DISCOVERY: THE HIDDEN MYSTEIES OF THE GRAND CANYON

First edition. October 4, 2024.

Copyright © 2024 Cassiel E. Nox.

ISBN: 979-8227011855

Written by Cassiel E. Nox.

Table of Contents

Kincaid's Discovery: The Hidden Mysteries of the Grand Canyon

Preface

Embark on a journey that transcends time and space, as we unravel one of the Grand Canyon's most captivating mysteries.

Kincaid's Discovery: The Hidden Mysteries of the Grand Canyon invites readers into a world where history dances with myth, and where discovery signals the start of a much deeper exploration. This book delves into the tale of G.E. Kincaid—a narrative marred by intrigue, speculation, and the enduring human quest for knowledge.

In writing this book, we sift through a century of storytelling, allowing each version of Kincaid's tale to illuminate the heart of a mystery that refuses to be conclusively solved. We examine the possibility that more lies beneath the narrative's surface, whether in the form of government secrecy, Indigenous wisdom, or the ingenious machinations of hoaxers. As you turn these pages, imagine yourself standing at the canyon's edge, contemplating the mysteries that might yet be uncovered, both in its breathtaking beauty and its hidden depths.

What drew me to this story was not just its drama, but its ability to stir deep questions about our history, our capacity for belief, and our inexhaustible fascination with the unknown. In these reflections, we find the real treasure—an invitation to look beyond the obvious and consider what stories and legacies are waiting to be unearthed.

Step with us into the shadows of the past and open your mind to the enduring spirit of exploration that Kincaid's mystery represents. Welcome to an adventure that transcends history and challenges the imagination.

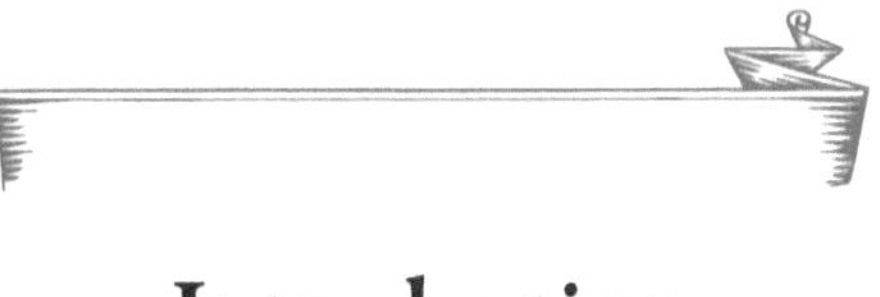

Introduction

In the vast and majestic expanse of the Grand Canyon, a story unfolds that blurs the line between history and legend. This is the tale of G.E. Kincaid and his alleged discovery of a mysterious cave—rumored to be filled with artifacts of Egyptian or Asian origin—deep within the Canyon's labyrinthine depths. The narrative captivates with its rich tapestry of intrigue, weaving together threads of exploration, cultural heritage, and tantalizing secrets that challenge our understanding of ancient civilizations.

Our journey begins in 1909, when the Arizona Gazette published a series of articles detailing Kincaid's audacious solo expedition down the Colorado River. What started as a daring adventure swiftly morphed into a tantalizing mystery, as the Gazette reported Kincaid's extraordinary claims of a vast man-made cave system filled with remarkable treasures and ancient mummies. For over a century, the world has been drawn to this enigmatic story, sparking debates among historians, archaeologists, and adventure seekers.

As we navigate the complexities of this historical mystery, we invite you to delve into the mix of archival newspaper reports, modern-day podcasts, and digital explorations that have kept the legends alive. Through the voices of skeptics and believers alike, we explore the varied explanations for Kincaid's claims, including the possibility of hoaxes and government cover-ups. The Grand Canyon, and the Kincaid legend it holds, continues to inspire curiosity and wonder, standing as a testament to the enduring allure of the undiscovered.

1. The Enigmatic Landscape of the Grand Canyon

1.1 Geological Formations and Their Significance

The Grand Canyon is more than a breathtaking vista; it is a magnificent tapestry of geological structures that tell the story of Earth's history over millions of years. Each layer of rock that lines the canyon walls carries with it not just minerals but a narrative of ancient environments, climatic shifts, and transformative geological events. The colorful strata—ranging from vibrant reds to muted grays—have been sculpted by the relentless forces of erosion and time, showcasing the processes that shaped not only this iconic landscape but our entire planet. Geologists and adventurers alike find themselves captivated by the way these unique formations reveal the power of natural forces at work, providing insights into the conditions that existed long before human beings walked the earth.

The rock layers of the Grand Canyon serve as a geological timeline, each stratum indicating a different chapter in the planet's history. The oldest rocks at the bottom, known as Vishnu Schist, date back nearly two billion years, sitting in stark contrast to the younger sedimentary rocks laid down around 270 million years ago. This diverse layering results from periods of volcanic activity, ancient seas, and shifting climates that have collided and converged through epochs. By understanding these layers, scientists can piece together the events that shaped the area and even draw parallels to other regions of the world. The study of these layers doesn't just reveal the past; it also allows for predictions about the future, offering valuable lessons on how our planet's environment may continue to change.

When you explore the Grand Canyon, you embark on a journey through time itself. Whether gazing up at the towering cliffs or pondering the formations below, it's important to consider how these geological wonders have inspired tales of ancient civilizations and theories that range from plausible to mysterious. For those walking along the trails, there is a practical tip to enhance the adventure: pay attention not only to the breathtaking views but also to the layers underfoot and consider their stories. Each step on this magnificent landscape is a step into the deep history of our Earth, encouraging reflection on our own place in the vast expanse of time.

1.2 The Role of Water in Shaping the Canyon

The process of erosion is a slow but powerful sculptor of landscapes, and the Colorado River has played a pivotal role in the formation of the Grand Canyon over millions of years. As the river sliced through the rock layers, it carried away sediment and transformed the terrain. This relentless flow of water, combined with the elements—wind and rain—created a magnificent chasm that not only reveals geological history but also tells the story of time itself. The river's journey is still observable today, meandering through the canyon while exposing fossils, minerals, and the intricate stratification of rock layers, which are witnesses to the Earth's geological past. Each part of the canyon reflects a different era, and as explorers navigate its depths, they unveil secrets locked in stone, shaped by the very water that sustains life along its banks.

Water continues to influence the canyon's ecosystem in profound ways. The Colorado River nourishes a diverse range of wildlife and plants that thrive along its banks, creating oases in the towering, arid expanse of rock and clay. This rich habitat is a stark contrast to the vast, dry surroundings, and it highlights the importance of water in sustaining life. Within the canyon, seasonal fluctuations in water flow can alter the landscape and influence patterns of erosion, revealing new facets of the rock formations. Additionally, as climate change impacts precipitation and river flow, the complexities of this ecosystem will only grow. The ongoing dance of water and land emphasizes not only the canyon's physical transformation but also the delicate balance that sustains its natural beauty and ecological health. Understanding this relationship invites reflection on our role in preserving such wonder.

Travelers to the Grand Canyon are encouraged to consider the profound history and mysteries that water reveals within this magnificent landmark.

Engaging with the landscape can amplify appreciation for the intricate interplay between erosion, the river, and the life it supports. For those adventurers who venture into the depths of the canyon, taking the time to observe how water shapes not only the land but also influences ecosystems offers a deeper connection to this natural wonder. Bring along a journal or sketchpad to capture impressions, thoughts, or even the changes you observe in the landscape as you cross paths with the ever-flowing Colorado River.

1.3 Biomes and Biodiversity: Life Within the Depths

The Grand Canyon is not just a stunning vista; it is a complex tapestry of ecosystems that have evolved over millions of years. Each layer of rock and soil creates a unique environment, offering a distinct habitat for myriad species. From the arid rim where hardy pines cling to cliff edges, to the lush riparian zones along the Colorado River, life manages to adapt in remarkable ways. Various biomes reveal themselves as one descends into the canyon, with each section showcasing its own set of flora and fauna. For instance, the sagebrush steppe at higher elevations transitions into the more diverse desert scrub. Visitors may notice how plant species, such as creosote and yucca, thrive in the sun-baked lands, while closer to the river, cottonwoods and willows find their niche in the moist soil. This diversity extends to the microhabitats that house unique organisms, demonstrating a web of life intricately connected to the canyon's geography.

Travelers to the Grand Canyon can enhance their experience by taking time to observe the varying ecosystems as they hike or raft through the depths. Understanding the intricate relationships among species, and their adaptations to such a majestic yet challenging environment, allows for a deeper appreciation of the canyon's beauty. Engaging with local conservation efforts or guided tours focused on ecology can further illuminate the significance of biodiversity in this iconic landscape. Remember, every step taken along the canyon not only reveals breathtaking views but also offers a glimpse into the intricate web that sustains life in one of nature's most extraordinary creations.

2. Ancient Inhabitants: A Glimpse into Prehistory

2.1 The Ancestral Puebloans: Origins and Lifestyle

The history of the Ancestral Puebloans is vibrant and layered, tracing their footsteps back thousands of years as they journeyed into the dramatic landscapes of the Grand Canyon region. Archaeological evidence suggests that these ancient peoples emerged from earlier cultures in the Southwest, possibly migrating into the area around A.D. 100. They settled near rivers, relying on the natural resources all around them. Their movements through canyons and plateaus were not just random; they were driven by a profound understanding of the land that offered both sustenance and shelter. Their advanced agricultural techniques, including the cultivation of maize, beans, and squash, reflects a sophisticated knowledge of horticulture that enabled them to thrive. Over time, this group honed their skills, creating a network of communities defined by their unique pottery styles, trade connections, and architectural innovations.

Daily life for the Ancestral Puebloans was rich and fulfilling, shaped by their environment and cultural practices. They built homes known as pueblos, which were constructed from stone and adobe, often nestled against cliff faces for protection against the elements. These multi-storied dwellings showcased their architectural prowess, with many featuring kivas, ceremonial spaces that served spiritual and community functions. In addition to farming, the Ancestral Puebloans engaged in skilled craftsmanship; their intricately designed pottery and woven textiles were not merely functional but also conveyed their stories and values. Social structures were integral to their communities, with kinship bonds and communal responsibilities guiding daily interactions. Festivals, ceremonies, and rituals punctuated their lives, linking them to their ancestors and the spiritual world. This engaged lifestyle cultivated a deep connection to their land and heritage, reflecting a society that revered nature's rhythms.

Understanding the Ancestral Puebloans offers valuable insights into the resilience and adaptability of human societies. Their legacy challenges modern perspectives about ancient cultures, inviting history enthusiasts and curious travelers alike to explore the landscapes that shaped their existence. Visiting sites like Mesa Verde or Canyon de Chelly can be a thought-provoking way to connect with these ancient peoples. These locations not only reveal remnants of their remarkable architecture and artistry but also speak to the stories of survival, innovation, and community that echo through time. Engaging with their history, whether through exploration or further study, provides a portal into a world that continues to offer lessons about sustainability and respect for the environment.

2.2 Artifacts of the Ancients: Tools and Technology

Canyon walls whisper secrets of a long-lost world, where the artifacts of ancient cultures emerge from the soil, revealing a tapestry of technological innovation. Among these artifacts, polished stone tools stand out as testaments to the ingenuity of the Ancestral Puebloans. Scrapers, blades, and arrowheads crafted from local materials not only demonstrate their resourcefulness but also hint at a sophisticated understanding of their environment. Each artifact, meticulously shaped and worn, tells a story of survival—whether it was the careful crafting of tools designed for hunting game or the creation of baskets that facilitated the gathering of wild plants. Engaging with these tools allows us to glimpse the everyday lives of those who once thrived in the vast landscapes of the Grand Canyon.

The significance of these tools goes beyond mere functionality; they offer insight into the daily survival practices of the Ancestral Puebloans, whose existence hinged on the ability to adapt to their environment. The efficient use of resources, as revealed through the artifacts, showcases a deep connection to the land and a knowledge of local flora and fauna. These tools were not just instruments; they were extensions of the people who made them, encapsulating their experiences, skills, and traditions. Through studying these artifacts, archaeologists can piece together the complex social structures, trade practices, and spiritual beliefs of these ancient societies. Each tool serves as a bridge to the past, invoking a sense of respect and wonder for those who walked before us.

As you explore the rugged trails of the Grand Canyon, consider the stories these artifacts tell. They prompt questions about human resilience and creativity, all while reminding us of the interconnectedness of cultures across time. Such reflections can enhance any journey through this majestic landscape, urging us to not only observe the natural beauty around us but to also ponder the lives and technologies of those who shaped this land long ago. For history enthusiasts and adventure seekers alike, the canyon offers a rich tapestry of discovery waiting to be unraveled, inviting everyone to engage with the mysteries hidden in its depths.

2.3 Spiritual Practices and Their Connection to the Canyon

The spiritual beliefs of the ancient inhabitants of the Grand Canyon are woven deeply into the fabric of the landscape. Their rituals often centered around the natural features of the canyon, which they viewed not merely as physical geographies but as sacred entities imbued with power and significance. They held various ceremonies connected to the river, the cliffs, and the vast sky, believing these elements were alive with spirits that influenced their lives. For them, the Great Spirit resided in every rock and river bend, and they would perform dances, songs, and offerings to honor these powerful forces. The emptiness of the canyon was not just void but a living, breathing presence, prompting rituals that reflected a deep respect and reverence for their surroundings.

This profound connection shaped their worldview, influencing how they interacted with nature. They viewed themselves as stewards of the land, responsible for maintaining harmony between their communities and the environment. Their spiritual practices fostered a sense of unity with the natural world, guiding their daily activities, agricultural practices, and even their social structures. Celebrations of the changing seasons, planting cycles, and animal migrations were opportunities to reaffirm their relationship with nature, imbuing everyday life with purpose and spirituality. This worldview cultivated a deep appreciation for the natural resources that sustained them, encouraging sustainable practices that would preserve the canyon's beauty for generations.

3. Myth and Legend: Stories of the Canyon

3.1 Native American Mythologies: Creation and Beyond

The Grand Canyon, a majestic chasm carved by the Colorado River, has captivated the imagination of countless visitors and observers. Within the depths of this natural wonder lies a rich tapestry of Native American myths that provide explanations for its creation. According to the Havasupai people, the Grand Canyon was formed when the trickster god, Coyote, sought to create a home for his people. In an act of mischief, he caused the earth to split open, revealing the depths of the canyon and providing a gateway to the spirit world. Another tribe, the Hopi, tells a story where the Grand Canyon is considered the entrance to the underworld, a sacred place where their ancestors emerged to inhabit the earth. These narratives serve not only to explain the canyon's physical presence but also to connect the people to their spiritual beliefs and the landscape itself, making every hike along its rim a journey through both history and mythology.

These stories are more than just colorful tales; they play a vital role in shaping cultural identity and imparting moral lessons. For many Native American tribes, myths and legends encompass values that guide behavior and community life. The lessons of respect for nature, the importance of harmony within the community, and the repercussions of greed and self-interest are woven into the fabric of these narratives. By recounting the tales of deities and ancestors, each generation reinforces its identity and connection to the land, ensuring that cultural wisdom is passed down. When visitors walk the trails of the Grand Canyon, they tread upon a landscape that embodies the stories of the past, inviting reflection on deeper truths about existence, connection, and the ongoing relationship between humanity and nature.

Understanding these myths can transform how one experiences the Grand Canyon, encouraging a sense of reverence for its beauty and history. Travel with an awareness of the stories that the land holds, seeking to learn and appreciate the culture that shaped it. Many organizations offer guided tours that delve into these narratives, enriching the experience by providing insights that might otherwise go unnoticed. Engaging with local communities, reading literature that explores these mythologies, or simply taking a moment to reflect on the connection between the stories and the natural world can deepen one's appreciation for this awe-inspiring landscape.

3.2 The Legends of the Hopi and Navajo Peoples

The vast canyons etched into the landscape of the American Southwest hold stories as ancient as the earth itself. For the Hopi and Navajo peoples, these remarkable formations are not mere geological wonders; they are woven into the very fabric of their legends. The Hopi speak of the Earth as a living being whose spirit is reflected in every rock and crevice. According to their beliefs, the Grand Canyon is a sacred place filled with stories of creation, involving Kachinas—spiritual beings who guide and teach. They believe that the canyons serve as a bridge between the physical and spiritual worlds, providing a canvas for rituals that honor ancestral ties and promote harmony with nature. Similarly, the Navajo tell tales of the Hero Twins, who traversed these vast landscapes facing numerous challenges, ultimately shaping the world and its features. Their legends echo the rich tapestry of their connection to the land, illustrating the belief that the canyon is alive with memories and lessons taught by their forebears.

As you explore the Grand Canyon and its surroundings, take a moment to appreciate the landscape not just as a marvel of nature but as a repository of stories and ancestral wisdom. Whether you are hiking the trails or simply sitting quietly to absorb the view, consider how the legends of the Hopi and Navajo peoples might reshape your understanding of this incredible place. Engaging with the land through the lens of these rich narratives can deepen your appreciation for the cultural heritage that defines this region, revealing that the beauty of the canyon reaches far beyond its breathtaking vistas.

3.3 The Influence of Oral Tradition on Canyon Culture

Oral storytelling plays a crucial role in preserving the rich history and vibrant culture associated with the Grand Canyon. Generations of ancestral voices weave narratives that capture the essence of this breathtaking landscape, transforming it from mere rock and water into a living tapestry of human experience. These stories often convey profound themes, including the relationship between nature and humanity, the sacredness of the land, and the trials and triumphs of those who have walked its trails. As anyone who has sat around a fire sharing stories knows, oral tradition has the power to connect people not just to each other but to their shared past. The tales of the canyon serve as a means to pass down knowledge and wisdom, ensuring that the cultural heritage remains alive in the hearts of the community. They remind us that history is not a static concept; rather, it is a dynamic force that continues to shape identities over time.

The influence of these oral traditions extends far beyond mere storytelling; they are foundational to social cohesion and community identity. In a region where diverse cultures intersect, oral narratives foster a sense of belonging and mutual understanding among villagers and clans. Each story told reinforces the bonds of kinship, as community members gather to recount shared experiences and lessons learned through generations. Through the act of storytelling, traditions are not only preserved but also adapted to contemporary contexts, allowing for the seamless integration of past and present. This shared practice creates a cultural fabric that enables individuals to view themselves as part of a larger narrative, one in which they contribute their own threads. The canyon emerges not just as a scenic backdrop but as a central character in the ongoing story of its people, offering both a refuge and a source of inspiration.

Understanding the significance of oral tradition in canyon culture invites deeper consideration of how we relate stories to our lives. The next time you explore the rugged trails of the Grand Canyon, take a moment to reflect on the voices of those who have come before you. Listen to the whisper of the wind against the cliffs and envision the tales that have been woven into that very landscape. Each step you take embodies a part of a living history—carry that thought with you, as it enhances the adventure of discovering this astonishing world.

4. Archaeological Explorations: Uncovering the Past

4.1 Major Discoveries in the Canyon

Significant archaeological findings have emerged from the depths of the Grand Canyon, shedding light on the lives of its ancient inhabitants. Among these discoveries, the remnants of settlements, tools, and ceremonial artifacts have revealed a rich tapestry of cultures that once thrived in this remarkable landscape. Excavations have uncovered pottery shards beautifully adorned with intricate designs, suggesting that these people had not only practical skills but also an artistic touch. Moreover, the discovery of ancient fire pits and food remnants indicates their resourcefulness and connection to the land. These findings paint a vivid picture of daily life and spiritual practices, suggesting a society deeply intertwined with the natural world.

Understanding the context of these discoveries is crucial for appreciating their significance. The artifacts tell a story of survival and adaptation, highlighting how ancient populations navigated the canyon's difficult terrain and harsh climate. Scholars emphasize these discoveries contribute profoundly

to our understanding of the historical narrative, extending our knowledge beyond the mere facts of who lived there. They open up pathways to explore cultural exchanges between different tribes, trade networks, and the shared knowledge that flowed through generations. In reflecting on these ancient societies, one realizes the complexity of their interactions with the environment, which resonated with spiritual significance and practical needs.

As you traverse the canyon, take a moment to ponder the lives that once flourished in this vast chasm. Consider visiting local museums or guided tours that focus on these archaeological findings. Engaging with the stories of the past can deepen your appreciation for the natural wonders around you, creating a connection between you and the ancient peoples who once called this majestic place home.

4.2 Modern Techniques in Archaeological Research

The realm of archaeology has witnessed remarkable technological advancements that have transformed how researchers delve into and interpret the complexities of ancient sites, particularly in challenging landscapes like the Grand Canyon. Equipped with cutting-edge tools such as geographical information systems (GIS), drones, and ground-penetrating radar (GPR), archaeologists can now map out vast areas with precision, revealing features that may lie hidden beneath the earth's surface. These technologies allow for aerial surveys that generate high-resolution topographic maps, providing crucial context for the sites being studied. The ability to conduct non-invasive scans means that researchers can gather information without disturbing the soils, preserving the integrity of the archaeological layers that hold secrets of the past.

Remote sensing has revolutionized the process of discovery in archaeology, offering a digital window into the subsurface features of the landscape. Techniques such as infrared imagery help detect variations in vegetation that indicate the presence of archaeological structures, while LIDAR technology can penetrate dense vegetation to reveal hidden ruins and pathways. These advancements not only enhance the likelihood of uncovering significant artifacts but also facilitate better documentation and comprehension of our ancient history. Excavation techniques have also evolved, with methodologies prioritizing meticulous material recovery and the careful interpretation of evidence. Stratigraphic excavation, for example, involves digging in layers to preserve artifacts in their original context, thus enabling a more accurate reconstruction of past human activity.

As adventure seekers approach the majestic Grand Canyon, they are not just greeted by breathtaking views but also by the whispers of history woven into its geological fabric. Understanding the modern techniques deployed in archaeological research encourages deeper insights into how ancient civilizations might have thrived in such an environment. Those interested in the mysteries of the past, especially in regions with rich histories, can embrace the idea that many secrets remain buried within these landscapes, waiting to be unveiled by the intersection of technology and dedicated scholarship. For those looking to explore these fields further, consider visiting local archaeological sites or participating in community archaeology projects, where you can experience firsthand how today's methods are reshaping our understanding of history.

4.3 The Ethics of Excavation: A Balancing Act

Understanding the ethical considerations surrounding the excavation and preservation of cultural artifacts is crucial in today's archaeological practices. Excavation isn't just about uncovering the past; it's about the responsibility that comes with it. Each artifact has a story, a cultural significance that connects communities, both past and present. The act of excavation often raises questions about ownership and representation. Who has the right to excavate these sites? The voices of indigenous communities must be prioritized. Their histories are an intrinsic part of the artifacts and sites being studied. Ethical excavation acknowledges the need to consult with these communities, respecting their beliefs and traditions, especially when it involves sacred sites or objects. It is a delicate dance of uncovering history while ensuring that the local cultures are honored and uplifted rather than overshadowed or exploited.

Archaeology walks a fine line between the pursuit of knowledge and the respect for indigenous rights and history. As scientists seek to unravel the mysteries of ancient civilizations, they must simultaneously engage with living cultures that still hold the heritage of these finds. This interaction often leads to a deeper understanding of the past, as indigenous perspectives can provide invaluable insights into how artifacts were created, used, and appreciated. Collaboration with local communities can enrich archaeological narratives, offering perspectives that pure empirical investigation might miss. Such cooperation may also touch on deeper philosophical questions: What does it mean to be caretakers of history? What obligations do contemporary societies have towards preserving not just artifacts but the stories and knowledge intertwined with them? These are ongoing conversations in modern archaeology as practitioners strive to balance academic curiosity with ethical responsibility.

For those looking to engagingly explore the complexities of this field, consider participating in local archaeological or cultural studies programs. Engaging directly with communities and professionals not only enhances the learning experience but also fosters a deeper respect for the histories being uncovered. Such practical experiences can illuminate the astonishing depth of cultural narratives while emphasizing the vital importance of ethical considerations in the excavation process.

5. Kincaid's Fabled Discovery: Fact or Fiction?

5.1 The Origins of Kincaid's Claims

Kincaid's claims emerged in the early 1900s, a time ripe with fascination for the unexplored and the extraordinary. The backdrop of this era saw a burgeoning interest in archaeology, driven by discoveries that brought to light the ancient civilizations of the Americas. The Grand Canyon, with its vast and rugged landscape, was more than just a natural wonder; it became a canvas upon which many stories were painted, including the tantalizing tales of hidden cities and lost treasures. Kincaid's assertion of discovering an ancient Egyptian-like temple deep within the canyon added layers to an already rich tapestry of narratives. At that time, many Americans were captivated by the idea that ancient cultures had left their marks in unexpected places. Influenced by a mix of romanticism and the spirit of discovery, Kincaid's narrative seemed to resonate with the imaginations of those searching for connections to a greater past.

The intrigue surrounding Kincaid's story was fueled by several cultural factors. The early 20th century was characterized by a growing fascination with the exotic, as the world became more interconnected, largely due to advances in transportation and communication. Stories of far-off places and ancient civilizations captivated audiences, prompting a sense of adventurous exploration. The notion of forgotten relics hidden in the American landscape captured the minds of not only explorers and archaeologists but also the general public. The Grand Canyon itself has often been seen as a mystical place, filled with echoes of past lives and cultural confluences. In this context, Kincaid's claims sparked imaginations, propelling discussions about life beyond the known and encouraging a reevaluation of what ancient cultures could reveal about humanity's journey.

As the echoes of Kincaid's claims resonate even today, exploring the Grand Canyon serves as a reminder that every rock and canyon could host untold stories, urging enthusiasts and travelers alike to remain open to the mysteries that the landscapes hold. Armed with this perspective, history enthusiasts venturing into such awe-inspiring territories should carry a sense of wonder and curiosity, always ready to embrace the adventure of discovery.

5.2 Analyzing the Evidence: What Archaeologists Found

The archaeological evidence relating to Kincaid's claims is a blend of intriguing discoveries and contested narratives. When Kincaid announced his findings of extensive tunnels and ancient structures in the Grand Canyon, he painted a picture of a lost civilization filled with treasures and advanced architecture. However, rigorous assessments by archaeologists revealed that many of these artifacts and formations were often exaggerated or misinterpreted. For instance, while some cave entrances were indeed located, evidence of an ancient civilization inhabiting these areas remained scant. Rocks and formations that seemed man-made turned out to be natural, shaped by millennia of erosion. As a result, the fine line between fact and fiction became increasingly blurred, making it essential for historians to sift through layers of myth to uncover the truth behind Kincaid's spectacular tales.

Modern archaeologists view Kincaid's discoveries with a critical but appreciative lens, acknowledging the excitement they stirred while also grounding them in a realistic framework. They consider his finds within a broader historical narrative that encompasses Native American histories and their rich ties to the Grand Canyon. Instead of searching for lost civilizations that Kincaid envisioned, researchers emphasize the importance of recognizing the longstanding heritage of Indigenous tribes like the Havasupai and the Hopi, who inhabited these lands long before Kincaid arrived. The mystery surrounding Kincaid's explorations evokes curiosity, yet it's vital to understand these findings against the backdrop of real cultures and histories that thrived in the region. By doing so, archaeologists strive to paint a more accurate picture of history that acknowledges both the allure of adventure and the reality of human existence in an ever-changing landscape.

For those interested in the tale of the Grand Canyon and its hidden secrets, exploring the stories of the Indigenous peoples could offer a deeper understanding of the region's past. Gathering knowledge from local guides or reading more about Indigenous histories can enrich one's journey through this awe-inspiring landscape, providing context beyond the sensationalized reports of early adventurers.

5.3 The Impact of Kincaid's Story on Popular Culture

Kincaid's narrative has significantly shaped how the Grand Canyon is portrayed in various forms of media, influencing public perceptions and sparking interest in both its natural beauty and its cultural history. His tale has weaved itself into the fabric of storytelling, from documentaries to novels, creating a vivid image of the canyon that blends adventure with mystery. The media often emphasizes Kincaid's descriptions of ancient civilizations, which has led to a fascination with the possibility of lost cultures that once thrived in this breathtaking landscape. This curiosity has prompted filmmakers to invest more in narratives that explore hidden treasures and archaeological enigmas, drawing audiences who yearn for adventure and connection to the past. Documentaries delve into the geology and ecological wonders of the canyon, frequently referencing Kincaid's interpretations, adding layers of intrigue to their explorations. As a result, the Grand Canyon has become a symbol of adventure and exploration, one where ancient history meets modern inquiry, inviting visitors and viewers alike to ponder its secrets.

The legacy of Kincaid's story is visible across many aspects of popular culture, particularly in literature and film. Writers have taken inspiration from his explorative narratives to create gripping tales set against the dramatic backdrop of the Grand Canyon. Novels that blend fiction with elements of historical exploration often cite Kincaid's findings, leading to narratives rich in adventure and deep in speculation. The cinematic world, too, has embraced his themes, creating films that are not just about the Grand Canyon's physicality but also about the mysteries lurking within. Adventure films and even documentaries frequently tap into the allure of Kincaid's discoveries, portraying characters who embark on quests for hidden artifacts or encounters with ancient spirits. These interpretations keep Kincaid's tale alive, continually feeding the public's imagination while promoting tourism and deeper engagement with the canyon itself.

Understanding the impact of Kincaid's story offers travelers a more profound experience as they journey through the vastness of the Grand Canyon. Visitors should consider not just the remarkable views, but also the stories that have woven themselves into the landscape. Engaging with local narratives, historical texts, and cultural studies allows one to appreciate the rich tapestry of myths and legends surrounding this iconic site. Whether exploring the trails or savoring the vistas, taking a moment to reflect on the intertwined stories of past explorers, including Kincaid, can transform a simple visit into an adventure filled with wonder and insight.

6. Conspiracy Theories: The Grand Canyon as a Vault

6.1 Theories of Hidden Civilizations Beneath the Surface

The Grand Canyon has long been at the center of many conspiracy theories and captivating tales of lost civilizations hidden within its majestic cliffs. Some enthusiasts point to ancient artifacts and unexplained structures reported by explorers and adventurers, fueling speculation about advanced societies that once thrived in the shadows of the canyon. These theories suggest that what lies beneath the surface may be more than just rock and soil; they imply a hidden world rich in history waiting to be uncovered. Stories of treasures, forgotten cities, and ancient knowledge have fascinated both the curious and the skeptical alike. Many assert that these civilizations, perhaps highly advanced and deeply spiritual, were deliberately concealed from mainstream history. The allure of ancient technologies and mystical practices motivates explorers and researchers to embark on journeys into the canyon's depths, searching for evidence of these enigmatic communities.

The cultural significance of these theories extends far beyond mere speculation. They shape collective imagination and public interest in archaeology and ancient history, inviting individuals to consider the unknown chapters of our past. As people encounter these stories, they are often drawn to the idea of untold miracles hidden in plain sight. The notion that civilizations, once vibrant and complex, exist just beneath the surface resonates with those who view the world through a lens of wonder and mystery. It provides an opportunity for adventure, reflection, and even a critique of accepted historical narratives, compelling us to ask critical questions about what we think we know. What if there are layers of history that still elude conventional understanding? By pondering these theories, society reconnects with its fascination for exploration while igniting conversations about the complexities of human existence throughout time.

6.2 Government Secrets and the Suppression of Knowledge

Claims of government cover-ups related to archaeological findings in the Grand Canyon have circulated for decades, capturing the imagination of history enthusiasts and conspiracy theorists alike. Some individuals believe that ancient artifacts, including advanced tools and remnants of unknown civilizations, were discovered within the canyon's depths, only to be purportedly concealed by federal authorities. Accounts from explorers and researchers suggest these discoveries challenge the established narratives of human history and the timeline of civilization. For instance, reports once claimed that mummies and intricate structures belonging to an ancient race were found, sparking debates about the legitimacy and significance of these findings. Many enthusiasts argue such artifacts could offer invaluable insights into American prehistory, yet they often feel dismissed by mainstream institutions. This perceived secrecy not only fuels curiosity but also fosters feelings of mistrust, as people question what information is being withheld and why.

The implications of these beliefs extend far beyond archaeological debates; they touch on societal trust in authorities and institutions. When the public encounters stories of hidden knowledge, it often leads to skepticism towards government bodies tasked with preserving and sharing historical narratives. The idea that potentially groundbreaking discoveries could be hidden away stirs a complex mixture of fear and fascination. Trust in historians, scientists, and the state begins to erode, as individuals feel alienated from the collective understanding of their past. This sentiment can culminate in broader movements advocating for transparency and unfettered access to information. As the Grand Canyon becomes not only a site of natural beauty but also a symbol of hidden truths, it prompts a reflective conversation about the nature of knowledge and the power dynamics that govern historical narratives.

This search for hidden truths leads adventurers and curious minds to explore the canyon and its surroundings, often seeking tales of lost civilizations and undisclosed artifacts. Travelers may visit archaeological sites, looking for clues about what has been uncovered and what might still lie undiscovered beneath the striking layers of rock. Engaging with the landscape and its mysteries creates an experience that transcends simple tourism; it becomes an adventure into the past and an inquiry into the present. By understanding the complexities of these government secrets and the narratives shaped by them, individuals can appreciate the rich tapestry of history while recognizing the importance of questioning what they are told. Those interested can start their journey by studying local archaeological projects supported by universities and museums, which aim to uncover the canyon's secrets through legitimate, scientific exploration.

6.3 The Role of Media in Shaping Perceptions

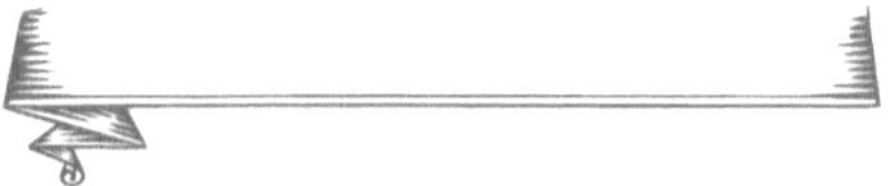

The portrayal of the Grand Canyon in various media forms has undergone noticeable changes throughout history, shaped by technological advancements and societal contexts. In the early 20th century, photographs and postcards emphasized its grandeur and natural beauty, often presenting it as a pristine American wilderness. Yet, with the rise of documentaries and films, the Canyon began to be infused with deeper narratives, including tales of ancient Native American cultures and early explorations. As the internet emerged, the Grand Canyon became a backdrop for a myriad of conspiracy theories ranging from ancient alien artifacts purportedly hidden within its depths to secret government experiments. These evolving portrayals reflect broader societal fascinations with the mystical and the unknown, as well as a desire to understand humanity's connection to such monumental natural wonders.

The advent of digital platforms has dramatically transformed how these narratives about the Grand Canyon are shared and received. Social media, blogs, and video-sharing sites allow users to disseminate information rapidly, bypassing traditional gatekeepers of knowledge. This democratization of information means that anyone with an internet connection can engage with or create content about the Grand Canyon, whether through personal anecdotes, drone footage, or speculative theories. As a result, the line between fact and fiction can become blurred, with conspiracy theories about the Canyon gaining traction alongside scientific discourse. This proliferation of content invites both excitement and skepticism as it fosters community discussions that can amplify both historical understanding and unfounded myths. Engaging with digital narratives, therefore, demands a critical eye and open mind, challenging us to discern truth amid a flood of information.

The richness of these narratives and the evolution of media portrayals continue to invite exploration and reflection. Understanding how the Grand Canyon is represented can lead to deeper questions about our perceptions of history and nature, as well as the stories we tell each other. While exploring the Canyon—whether in person or through the lens of a screen—consider seeking out multiple sources and perspectives. This approach can offer a fuller picture of the Canyon's significance, enrich your knowledge about ancient civilizations and contemporary cultures, and deepen your appreciation for this natural wonder.

7. The Canyon's Natural Wonders: A Geological Timeline

7.1 The Formation of the Canyon: A Geological Perspective

The Grand Canyon, a colossal chasm carved into the heart of the American Southwest, is a testament to the relentless forces of nature over millions of years. Its formation is a complex tapestry woven from geological events that date back nearly two billion years. The story begins with the ancient rocks, primarily composed of metamorphic and igneous formations, deposited in a time when this region was submerged under oceans and dominated by volcanic activity. Over eons, sedimentary layers built upon these older rocks, creating a thick crust. As tectonic plates shifted and collided, the earth's crust buckled and folded, leading to the uplift that created the Colorado Plateau. This significant geological raise exposed these layers to the forces of erosion.

Water, wind, and ice played crucial roles in shaping the Grand Canyon into its current form. The Colorado River, carving its path through the plateau, acted like a sculptor, eroding rock and soil with tremendous power. This process is not merely linear; it is punctuated by periods of climate change, which caused fluctuations in river flow and sediment deposition. Each layer of sediment tells a story—of ancient seas, desert landscapes, and forests—that contribute to the canyon's rich tapestry of geological history. Understanding these processes reveals the dynamic nature of our planet's surface, reminding us that the Earth is always changing, continually revealing its history through such awe-inspiring formations.

The significance of the Grand Canyon's geological processes extends beyond mere aesthetics; it provides a tangible record of the Earth's geological history. Each stratum within the canyon offers insight into the environmental conditions and biological life that existed at different points in time. For enthusiasts of history and archaeology, the canyon is not only a natural wonder but also a visible narrative of the earth's evolutionary timeline. Additionally, the exploration of ancient civilizations that once thrived in the surrounding regions highlights the deep connection between geology and human history. One can ponder how indigenous tribes, for whom the canyon holds sacred meaning, interpreted its vastness. The intertwining of cultural narratives and geological processes creates a rich backdrop for reflection. Whether traversing its rim or standing on its floor, visitors to the Grand Canyon cannot help but feel a profound sense of awe and an urge to explore the layers of both earth and history that lie before them, making it a captivating destination for both the adventurous and the reflective.

7.2 The Role of Erosion: Nature's Sculpting Tool

Erosion is a fundamental force in shaping landscapes, and nowhere is this more apparent than in the Grand Canyon. Over millions of years, water, wind, and ice have worked in concert to carve deep gorges and stunning rock formations. The process begins with rainfall, which moves across the land, collecting and forming rivers that relentlessly cut into the earth. The Colorado River, the artery of the canyon, flows with determination, slicing through hard rock layers and transporting sediment downstream. Meanwhile, wind whips through crevices, wearing away softer materials and reshaping cliffs with each passing gust. Even ice plays a role; as winter approaches, it seeps into cracks in the rock, freezing and expanding, ultimately fracturing the stone. Together, these forces create a dynamic interplay, continuously reshaping the canyon

and revealing layers of geological history.

The future of the canyon's landscape is uncertain, as ongoing erosion will continue to change its features. Climate change poses a new challenge, with altered precipitation patterns affecting water flow in the Colorado River. Increased temperatures may lead to more evaporation and less runoff, potentially slowing the erosion process. However, the existing erosion has already set into motion the transformation of the canyon's terrain, which could result in new formations appearing while others disappear. This constant metamorphosis leaves us pondering how the canyon—one of nature's most impressive monuments—will look in centuries to come. The mysterious rhythms of erosion remind us of our impermanence, inviting us to reflect on the cycles of nature and our fleeting moments within them. Exploring this ancient landscape today offers a glimpse into the power of time and the silent artistry of wind and water.

Understanding the forces of erosion can enrich your visit to the Grand Canyon. By observing how different elements harmonize to shape this iconic landscape, you can gain a deeper appreciation for the environment. Take a moment to notice the rock layers as you hike; each stratum tells a story of the earth's long history. Bring a journal to jot down your thoughts on the features you encounter or the history you've learned. Embrace the adventure of discovering this natural wonder and reflect on the delicate balance of forces that have sculpted not just the canyon but also our very existence.

7.3 Dramatic Events: Earthquakes and Flooding

Significant geological events, particularly earthquakes and floods, have played a crucial role in shaping the Grand Canyon over millions of years. The shifting tectonic plates and volcanic activity beneath the earth's surface have caused powerful earthquakes that altered the landscape drastically. Each seismic event contributed to the canyon's depth and breadth, carving out new pathways through the rock and presenting a constantly changing topography. Flood events, especially those caused by rapid snowmelt or heavy rains, have also sculpted the canyon's features. The Colorado River, which winds its way through the canyon, has frequently overflowed its banks, reshaping sediment deposits and eroding cliffs. The formidable power of water has cut through layers of rock, revealing geological histories that span back over two billion years.

These dramatic events illustrate the dynamic nature of the Grand Canyon; it is not a static monument of nature, but one in a continual state of transformation. The interplay of geological forces becomes a story of resilience and adaptation, not just for the land but for the flora and fauna that call this incredible place home. Adventure seekers and explorers are drawn to these changes, eager to witness firsthand the aftermath of natural disasters that sculpted this majestic landscape. Each canyon wall silently tells a tale of its fierce past, inviting reflection on the impermanence of nature itself. The ever-present potential for future earthquakes and floods reminds us that the canyon's evolution is far from over, presenting both a challenge and an invitation for those who venture into its depths.

Understanding the impact of these geological events can enhance your visit to the Grand Canyon, making it more than just a scenic destination. When planning your exploration, consider embarking on guided tours that focus on the geology of the area. Knowledgeable guides can provide insights into how specific events shaped the canyon you see today, enriching your experience and igniting a deeper appreciation for this natural wonder.

MODERN ADVENTURERS

8. Travelers through Time: The Grand Canyon in History

8.1 Early European Explorers and Their Accounts

The narratives of early European explorers reveal a fascinating tapestry of their impressions of the Grand Canyon. During the 16th and 17th centuries, these adventurers embarked on daring expeditions, primarily driven by the lure of discovery and wealth. Figures such as García López de Cárdenas, who is credited with the first European sighting of the Grand Canyon in 1540, crafted vivid descriptions of the canyon's immense beauty and majestic cliffs. His account captured the breathtaking layers of red rock and the vast expanse of the canyon, igniting imaginations far beyond the borders of the New World. Explorers often penned their impressions with a mix of awe and trepidation, portraying the canyon as both an alluring landscape and an intimidating frontier, fraught with the unknown.

The accounts of these early explorers significantly shaped Western perceptions of the Grand Canyon and its indigenous peoples. The explorers, while marveling at the canyon's grandeur, often presented a perspective colored by their cultural biases and objectives. Their writings tended to describe Native American tribes as primitive or mystical, perspectives that sometimes romanticized their existence but also contributed to pervasive stereotypes. This portrayal affected how society viewed both the canyon and its original inhabitants. The explorers' mix of admiration and condescension created a narrative that persisted in Western thought, framing the canyon not just as a physical space, but also as a cultural symbol entangled with ideas of civilization versus wilderness. Such explorations left a legacy that continues to influence how we engage with and understand the Grand Canyon today.

Delving into the diaries and journals of these adventurers offers a unique lens to understand the intersection of exploration and cultural perception.

Engaging with these texts can provide valuable insights into the historical context and mindset of early European explorers. Visitors to the Grand Canyon can enrich their experience by exploring the history behind its discovery. A practical tip for travelers is to visit local museums and historical sites that showcase these narratives, allowing a deeper connection with the land and its storied past.

8.2 The Grand Canyon in American Literature

The Grand Canyon has long captivated the imaginations of artists, writers, and thinkers, serving as a profound symbol in American literature. Its majestic cliffs and vast expanse reflect the beauty and brutality of nature, embodying themes such as adventure, introspection, and the sublime. Authors have often used the canyon as a backdrop to explore the human condition, our place in the universe, and the connection between civilization and the natural world. In works ranging from John Wesley Powell's explorations to the vivid poetry of contemporary writers, the Grand Canyon emerges as a character in its own right, evoking a sense of wonder and the mysteries of existence. This literary portrayal reveals not only a geographical marvel but also a deeper metaphor for life's journey, the passage of time, and the enduring spirit of exploration that defines American culture. The canyon compels readers to reflect on their own experiences and the narratives that shape their understanding of the world.

Several significant literary works have contributed to the rich mythos surrounding the Grand Canyon. For instance, in the late 19th century, John Muir's writings illustrated the grandeur of the canyon while advocating for conservation, illuminating the spiritual and emotional resonance of nature. Similarly, the poignant descriptions found in Edward Abbey's Desert Solitaire evoke a profound sense of solitude and reverence for the landscape, framing the canyon not only as a beautiful escape but also as a place of personal introspection and enlightenment. Other authors like Zane Grey captured the adventurous spirit of the West through tales that intertwine the rugged wilderness with the human experience. As these literary voices blend adventure with philosophical inquiry, the canyon transforms into an archetype of exploration and self-discovery, drawing readers into a dialogue about nature, identity, and the unknown. Each narrative contributes layers to the canyon's complexity, allowing it to remain a timeless emblem within American literature.

To truly appreciate the depth of the Grand Canyon's literary significance, one can visit its stunning vistas and contemplate the words of those who have sought inspiration from its stones. Engaging with both the landscape and the stories it has inspired can deepen your understanding of the canyon's role in shaping not only literature but also the American spirit itself. Carry a journal on your journey, and allow the breathtaking views to kindle your creativity, just as they have for so many writers before you.

8.3 Modern Adventurers: Hiking and River Rafting

Modern adventurers are drawn to the Grand Canyon with an insatiable curiosity and a desire for both challenge and discovery. Hikers, equipped with rugged boots and backpacks filled with necessities, tackle the trails that wind through this vast chasm carved by the Colorado River. Some set out from the South Rim, where panoramic views entice them with their beauty, while others brave the more secluded paths of the North Rim. These adventurers often share stories of the majestic vistas and the wild encounters that await them, from valuable sightings of bighorn sheep to the delicate flora that clings to the rock faces. Meanwhile, river rafters seek the thrill of navigating the turbulent waters below, guided by experienced outfitters who know the river's twists and turns. They face the exhilarating rapids that challenge their skills and bravery, all while enveloped in the canyon's awe-inspiring landscape. The camaraderie among fellow adventurers creates lasting connections as they encounter the majestic cliffs, hidden caves, and sacred Native American sites that resonate with history.

Adventure tourism significantly influences the culture and economy surrounding the Grand Canyon. As more visitors flock to this natural wonder, local businesses thrive, offering everything from gear rentals to guided tours. This influx of tourism fosters a sense of community pride among residents who share their knowledge of the area's rich history and ecology. However, it also raises critical questions about sustainability and the preservation of the canyon's delicate ecosystem. While economic benefits are apparent, challenges such as overcrowding and environmental degradation loom. Community efforts to balance tourism and conservation are becoming increasingly essential, highlighting the importance of respecting the ancient sacred spaces that have long been part of the Native American heritage. The canyon becomes not just a playground for thrill-seekers but a canvas where culture, history, and nature intertwine, encouraging all who visit to reflect on their impact.

Exploring the Grand Canyon by foot or by raft reveals layers of history that are rich and complex. Adventurers who traverse these paths witness not only the scenery but also the traces of ancient civilizations that once thrived in the region. The remnants of prehistoric peoples, evidenced by petroglyphs and artifacts scattered throughout the canyon, add a layer of mystery to the experience. Understanding these connections enhances the adventure, urging travelers to appreciate the cultural tapestry woven into the land. A practical tip for anyone planning to embark on a journey through the Grand Canyon is to consider starting early in the day, especially for hiking. The temperatures can rise quickly, and catching the sunrise over the canyon offers a breathtaking experience that few forget.

9. Environmental Challenges: Preservation Efforts

9.1 The Impact of Tourism on the Canyon's Ecosystem

The Grand Canyon is a stunning natural wonder that captures the imagination of millions of visitors each year. However, the surge in tourism has profound effects on this delicate ecosystem. As people flock to experience the breathtaking views and unique geological formations, the environment faces significant pressure. Foot traffic along trails, pollution from litter, and the disturbance of wildlife habitats are just a few consequences that can disrupt the balance of the canyon's natural systems. The increasing number of tourists often leads to soil erosion, trampling of native plants, and alterations to water quality as more visitors utilize the area's resources. Each footprint can leave a mark, and as more people explore this majestic landscape, it becomes essential to understand the fragility of the ecosystems that exist within it.

Finding a balance between promoting tourism and practicing environmental stewardship is crucial for the preservation of the Grand Canyon. Conservation efforts must be strengthened as the need for access and enjoyment of this national treasure grows. Environmental education plays a vital role; when visitors understand the importance of preserving the canyon's ecosystem, they can engage in more responsible behaviors. Programs that encourage sustainable tourism practices, such as guided hikes that minimize impact, can help mitigate the negative effects of enormous crowds. Only by fostering a culture of respect and awareness regarding the delicate ecosystems of the canyon can we ensure future generations will explore its wonders. Tourists are called to be not just visitors but stewards of this ancient land, emphasizing that everyone holds a piece of the responsibility for its care.

When planning a visit to the Grand Canyon, consider choosing off-peak times to explore its trails and viewpoints. This small change can significantly ease the strain on the ecosystem and enhance your experience in solitude.

Engaging with local conservation programs can further enrich your understanding of the landscape, allowing you to appreciate the canyon not just as a destination but as a living, breathing entity deserving of protection.

9.2 Conservation Efforts: Who's Protecting the Canyon?

The Grand Canyon, a breathtaking marvel carved by the Colorado River, is the focus of dedicated efforts by a myriad of organizations and passionate individuals committed to its survival and preservation. Among these are the National Park Service, which oversees the canyon as part of the national park system, and non-profits like the Grand Canyon Conservancy that raise funds and awareness about the canyon's unique environment and cultural significance. Local indigenous tribes, such as the Havasupai and Hualapai, also play a significant role, advocating for the protection of their ancestral lands and sharing their rich cultural heritage with visitors. Scientists, researchers, and volunteers collaborate in various programs aimed at monitoring wildlife and restoring native plant species, forging a collective mission to sustain the natural balance of this iconic landscape.

Success stories form the backbone of conservation initiatives at the Grand Canyon. Programs that focus on habitat restoration and the reintroduction of native species have shown remarkable results, reviving ecosystems once threatened by invasive species and human activities. Geological surveys and archaeological studies continue to unearth valuable insights into ancient civilizations that once thrived in this vast region, allowing for a deepened understanding of the land's history. Moreover, educational outreach programs engage the public to inspire future generations to cherish and safeguard this natural wonder. These initiatives not only protect the canyon's biodiversity and cultural heritage, but also foster a sense of stewardship among visitors, encouraging them to participate in preservation efforts.

Visitors to the Grand Canyon can actively contribute to these conservation efforts simply by choosing responsible tourism practices. Opting for guided tours offered by companies that emphasize ecological sustainability can help reduce human impact on the environment. Additionally, participating in organized volunteer projects during your visit can provide firsthand experience in preserving this unique landscape. Awareness and adoption of Leave No Trace principles will further ensure that the Grand Canyon remains a majestic resource for generations to come.

9.3 Climate Change: Threats to the Grand Canyon

The Grand Canyon, a striking landscape carved over millions of years, is witnessing the profound effects of climate change, which threaten its unique environment and diverse biodiversity. The rising temperatures alter precipitation patterns, leading to extended periods of drought that affect not just the vegetation, but also the intricate web of wildlife that relies on it. Native species, like the bighorn sheep and various plants found only in this region, face increased stress as their habitats change. In addition, invasive species, more resilient to changing weather conditions, encroach upon native habitats, pushing out local flora and fauna and disrupting delicate ecosystems. The shifts in climate also lead to more frequent and intense weather events, such as floods and wildfires, further jeopardizing the canyon's rich cultural and natural heritage.

Future scenarios paint a concerning picture for the Grand Canyon and its ecosystems. If current trends continue, some species may face extinction while others may move into areas that cannot support them, leading to a domino effect throughout the ecosystem. The importance of adaptive conservation strategies becomes increasingly clear in this context. These strategies can include the restoration of native habitats, controlled burns to prevent larger wildfires, and initiatives to reduce human impact on the landscape. Engaging local communities in conservation efforts and embracing sustainable tourism practices are crucial steps. By understanding the interconnectedness of life in the canyon, we can foster a sense of responsibility and stewardship towards this natural wonder, ensuring it remains a thriving ecosystem for generations to come.

Visitors to the Grand Canyon can contribute to conservation efforts simply by being mindful of their impact. Staying on marked trails, respecting wildlife, and minimizing waste can help preserve the beauty and integrity of this incredible place. Engaging with local ranger programs and educational initiatives can provide deeper insights into the changing environment, fostering a collective movement towards protecting one of nature's greatest masterpieces.

10. Reflection and Inspiration: Artistic Interpretations of the Canyon

10.1 The Canyon in Visual Arts: Paintings and Photography

Over the centuries, the Grand Canyon has inspired artists from various backgrounds and artistic movements to capture its breathtaking beauty through numerous mediums. Early depictions began with native tribes, who painted the canyon onto pots and cliff walls, sharing their spirituality and connection to the land. In the 19th century, the American West was a subject of fascination, enticing painters like Thomas Moran, whose vibrant canvases captured the mesmerizing layers of rock and the interplay of light across the canyon. His work, rooted in romanticism, portrayed the Grand Canyon as a site of awe, blending color and emotion to convey the beauty of the landscape. Photographers like Ansel Adams later revolutionized the representation of the canyon, bringing new techniques and a focus on reality that captivated the public imagination. His black-and-white images fought hard against the elements of time, showcasing the majesty of the canyon and its intricate details

that often went unnoticed. These artists, each from different eras and perspectives, have paved a rich narrative that documents humanity's relationship with this natural wonder.

The interplay between artistic interpretation and the natural beauty of the Grand Canyon invites contemplation about how perception shapes reality. Artists do not merely reproduce what they see; they embed their emotions, thoughts, and even societal values into their works. This interpretation introduces a layering of meaning beyond the physical landscape. For example, landscapes painted during the nineteenth century not only glorified the untouched wilderness but also represented the idea of Manifest Destiny and the American spirit. Likewise, contemporary artists often engage with themes of environmentalism and conservation, reflecting society's evolving relationship with nature. Each painting or photograph captures a moment in time, an emotion, and a viewpoint, urging viewers to reflect on the marriage between natural beauty and human experience. Such artistic representations challenge observers to reconsider what they perceive and feel, provoking questions about our roles in preserving the surrounding wonders.

When exploring the Grand Canyon, consider its artistic interpretations as part of your journey. Observing how different artists approached this magnificent landscape can enhance your experience, providing a deeper understanding of its significance beyond mere visual beauty. Take a moment to appreciate that each viewpoint along the rim may be transformed into a canvas of your own imagination, echoing the sentiments of those who have captured it before you. With a sketchbook in hand or a camera at your side, you can record your personal narrative of the canyon, contributing to its long-standing legacy as a muse for creativity and reflection.

10.2 Literature Inspired by the Grand Canyon

Numerous literary works have drawn from the grandeur and mystique of the Grand Canyon, capturing its essence in vivid prose and poetry. Authors like Edward Abbey and Mary Hunter Austin have transported readers through their evocative descriptions that paint the canyon in both physical and spiritual dimensions. Abbey's Desert Solitaire articulates a deep connection to the land and explores the philosophy of nature through personal reflection amidst the labyrinth of canyons and rock formations. Similarly, Austin's The Land of Little Rain uses the canyon's landscapes to convey the beauty and harshness of the desert, intertwining the thoughts of humanity with the ancient geological narratives told through time. These literary works not only highlight the canyon as a destination but also reflect its impact on the human soul, transforming a mere geographic location into a space of introspection and adventure.

These narratives extend beyond sheer beauty; they enhance our understanding of the Grand Canyon's cultural significance. They provide a lens through which we can view the historical interplay between indigenous peoples and their sacred lands. Literary explorations often touch upon the spiritual resonance that the canyon holds for various Native American tribes, emphasizing their ancient ties to the land and their stories that echo through the canyon's vastness. Such works challenge readers to contemplate the canyon's role not only as a natural wonder but as a repository of history and culture. Exploring the canyon through literature allows one to engage with its mysteries, diving into questions about conservation, identity, and our relationship with the natural world. This reflection enriches our collective narrative, linking past civilizations, modern adventures, and the enduring charm of one of nature's grandest spectacles.

For those visiting the Grand Canyon, delving into literature inspired by its landscapes can enhance the experience. Reading about the canyon's rich history and diverse ecosystem before embarking on your journey can deepen your appreciation for what you see. Many books provide insights that enhance the journey, suggesting which areas to explore not just for their beauty but for their stories. By carrying a novel or collection of essays that speak to the canyon's spirit, you invite into your adventure a sense of wonder that connects the past with the present, enriching your understanding of this majestic landscape.

10.3 Music and Dance: Expressions of the Canyon Experience

Composers and choreographers have long been inspired by the natural wonder of the Grand Canyon. The vastness of its landscape, the interplay of light and shadow, and the symphony of sounds from the rustling wind and flowing rivers evoke a potent canvas for artistic interpretation. When creating music inspired by the canyon, artists often draw on its majestic silence and unexpected bursts of overwhelming beauty. They weave together melodies that mimic the meandering trails and the soaring heights of the canyon walls. Likewise, choreographers translate the essence of the canyon into dynamic movements that capture the force of the Colorado River carving through the rock, as if each step traveled within the dance itself reflects a journey into this monumental space. This exploration can involve the incorporation of traditional Indigenous sounds or contemporary styles that echo the canyon's rich cultural tapestry. Integrating nature's elements into these art forms evokes not just a representation of the landscape but also an invitation into a deeper understanding of its narrative.

Emotional resonance plays a vital role in how music and dance convey the grandeur of the Grand Canyon. Artistic expressions often stir in the audience a sense of wonder, awe, and contemplation, mirroring the feelings evoked by the canyon itself. When a composer evokes the echoing majesty of the canyon in their music, listeners may feel transported to that expansive space, experiencing the call of the wild and the timelessness of nature. Similarly, dancers express the emotional weight of their movements, inviting observers to connect with the rhythms of the earth and invoke the canyon's soulful presence. The art forms can even provoke reflections on human existence in relation to nature, as artists portray the struggle and triumph inherent in the rugged terrain. Whether through a haunting melody or a graceful dance, the emotional depth captured in these artistic interpretations fosters a renewed appreciation for the Grand Canyon, encouraging audiences to explore their inner landscapes while they journey through this natural wonder.

As you prepare to experience the Grand Canyon yourself, consider visiting during different times of day to fully appreciate the variations in light and color, which can influence the way musicians and dancers interpret its essence. Early morning or late afternoon, for example, offers a unique perspective on the canyon's grandeur, as the changing light creates a dramatic play of shadows that artists often strive to capture. Being in tune with the shifts in your surroundings may inspire your own reflections on the natural world, enhancing your understanding of the artistic expressions that arise from this remarkable landscape.

11. The Intersection of

Science and Spirituality

11.1 The Canyon as a Site for Spiritual Experiences

The Grand Canyon holds profound spiritual significance for many indigenous cultures, particularly for tribes like the Havasupai, Hopi, and Navajo. For these communities, the canyon is not just a stunning geographical feature; it embodies the stories, traditions, and sacred history that shape their identities. The deep ravines and towering cliffs are seen as the remnants of their ancestral spirits, and the landscape often plays a crucial role in their spiritual practices and ceremonies. Visitors who come to the canyon often feel an electric energy in the air, as though the very rocks are whispering secrets of the past. This sense of reverence can foster a deep appreciation for the sacredness of nature and inspire individuals to connect with something greater than themselves. Understanding the canyon through this cultural lens invites all who visit to reflect on their own place within the vast tapestry of existence.

Many visitors to the Grand Canyon report transformative experiences that deepen their relationship with nature. Standing at the rim, facing the expansive views of layered rock and vibrant colors, individuals often feel a sense of awe that sparks introspection. It is not uncommon for people to experience moments of clarity or heightened awareness as they absorb the beauty surrounding them. Some describe feelings of unity with the earth; the canyon somehow reminds them of their own life journeys, struggles, and the greater forces at play in the world. For some, hiking along the trails leads to quiet moments of contemplation, allowing thoughts to flow freely like the Colorado River carving through the canyon. These personal revelations can leave a lasting impact, motivating travelers to seek authenticity in their own lives and to appreciate the delicate balance of nature.

The Grand Canyon serves as more than just a visual spectacle; it acts as a canvas for personal and collective histories filled with mystery and adventure. Taking time during a visit to reflect, meditate, or simply breathe in the beauty can enhance one's experience and understanding of this natural wonder. Carrying a sense of respect and mindfulness can help in embracing the canyon's rich heritage and the spiritual journeys that it continues to inspire.

11.2 Scientific Inquiry and Philosophical Questions

The Grand Canyon stands as a majestic testament to nature's artistry, carved over millions of years, its layers revealing the story of our planet. As scientists explore this vast geological wonder, they uncover not only the intricacies of rock formations and fossil records but also the profound philosophical questions that arise from such exploration. What does it mean to exist amid such timeless beauty? The sheer scale of the canyon often evokes a sense of humility and wonder in visitors and researchers alike, prompting reflections on human existence in relation to the grand tapestry of life that the canyon represents. This becomes especially poignant when one considers the deep time represented in its walls, where each stratum offers a glimpse into epochs long gone. As scientists study the canyon, they find themselves not merely exploring the earth but also grappling with questions about the nature of time, the fragility of human life, and our place in the universe.

The dialogue between scientific inquiry and spiritual beliefs surrounding the Grand Canyon is rich and multifaceted. Native American tribes, such as the Havasupai and Hopi, view the canyon as sacred ground, intertwined with their creation stories and cultural identity. For them, the canyon is not just a geological formation but a living entity, steeped in ancestral significance. This belief often contrasts with the objective lens of scientific exploration, which seeks to understand the canyon through empirical evidence and analysis. Yet, these two perspectives do not have to be at odds. Instead, they can complement one another, offering a holistic view of the canyon that encompasses both the material and spiritual realms. As researchers engage with indigenous wisdom and modern geological techniques, they uncover a richer narrative that honors both the data of science and the depth of human experience.

When visiting the Grand Canyon, consider approaching this natural wonder with both curiosity and respect. Engage with both the scientific interpretive guides and the stories shared by local tribes. This blend of knowledge can deepen your appreciation for the canyon, allowing you to reflect on the complex interplay of time, nature, and humanity. Always remember to leave no trace, preserving this magnificent landscape for future generations to ponder and explore its mysteries.

11.3 Cultivating Respect: Balancing Belief and Knowledge

Respecting both scientific knowledge and indigenous belief systems in the Grand Canyon is crucial for a deeper engagement with this breathtaking landscape. Scientific insights provide valuable information about the geological formations, ecosystems, and archaeological sites that make the canyon a rich repository of history. Researchers have spent years studying the layers of rock that tell stories of ancient environments, about the climate changes that shaped this iconic site, and how human activity intertwined with nature over thousands of years. At the same time, the wisdom and narratives held by Indigenous tribes, such as the Havasupai and Hopi, bring a unique tapestry of cultural significance to the Grand Canyon. These stories often encompass spiritual connections to the land, offering context that numerical data alone cannot convey. Both realms of understanding—scientific exploration and indigenous knowledge—can coexist, creating a fuller picture of the canyon's importance and allowing for a more holistic appreciation of its heritage.

The balance between these different forms of knowledge can significantly enrich our understanding of the Grand Canyon, revealing layers beyond what is visible to the eye. When we respect Indigenous beliefs, we open ourselves to narratives that speak to the canyon as a living entity, one that has guided human existence for generations. These perspectives can invite visitors to engage in a deeper reflection about their own relationship with nature and history. Exploring the canyon with both its scientific facts and indigenous stories in mind fosters a sense of adventure and discovery that is more profound than simply witnessing the geological marvels. Such a balanced approach encourages us to think critically and empathetically about how we relate to the places we visit and the histories they hold.

By actively seeking to understand this duality of knowledge, travelers can enhance their experiences in the Grand Canyon. Before visiting, consider researching the local Indigenous narratives and the scientific discoveries made in the area. This preparation will enrich your journey, allowing you to appreciate the canyon not just as a stunning natural wonder, but as a sacred site with its own vibrant culture and history. Engaging with both scientific and indigenous perspectives transforms a simple hike into a meaningful exploration of humanity's connection to the land.

12. The Role of Water: Life and Culture in the Canyon

12.1 The Colorado River: Lifeblood of the Canyon

The Colorado River serves as the essential artery for the Grand Canyon, shaping not only the unique landscape but also sustaining a rich tapestry of life. For countless generations, this river has been the lifeblood of the region's ecosystem. It provides the necessary hydration to flora and fauna that have adapted to the arid climate surrounding the canyon. The lush riparian zones, with their diverse plant life and vital habitats, depend on this singular waterway. Beyond its ecological significance, the river holds great importance for indigenous peoples who have called these canyons home long before the advent of modern civilization. For these communities, the Colorado River is more than just water; it has been a source of sustenance, a means of transportation, and an integral part of their cultural identity. Their spiritual connections to the river highlight its role far beyond the material, revealing the mysteries and stories that echo through the canyon walls.

The influence of the Colorado River extends into daily life, culture, and recreation for all who dwell within and visit the canyon. Its waters shape the recreational activities that attract adventure seekers from all over the world. Rafting through the canyon is not merely a thrilling endeavor; it offers a unique perspective of the terrain and allows travelers to engage with the stunning beauty of this ancient landscape. The river's presence fosters a connection with the past, as modern explorers often find themselves retracing the routes of those who came before them. The multifaceted relationship that people have with the Colorado River intertwines with the storytelling traditions of the region, where tales of exploration, survival, and harmony with nature echo through time. This interplay of water, land, and culture continues to inspire those who seek adventure and understanding within the vast geological grandeur of the Grand Canyon.

Visitors to the Grand Canyon should consider taking a moment to listen to the sounds of the river and reflect on its journey. Each ripple carries with it centuries of history and the whispers of countless lives connected to its flow. Engaging with the beauty of the Colorado River provides a deeper appreciation not only for the landscape but also for the cultures that have thrived along its banks.

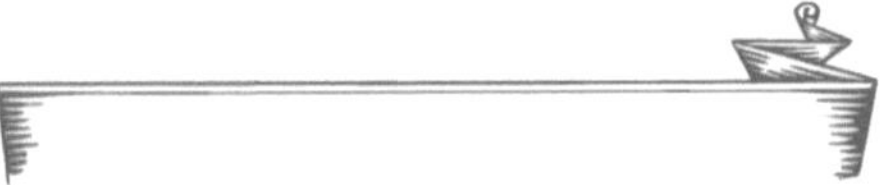

12.2 Water Management: Ancestral Practices and Modern Challenges

Indigenous communities across the globe have developed ingenious methods for managing water resources that have persisted through centuries. These traditional approaches are deeply intertwined with cultural practices and the spiritual significance of water as a life-giving force. For example, the Pueblo tribes of the American Southwest utilized techniques like rainwater harvesting and the construction of check dams to capture and direct water through arid landscapes. They understood the importance of seasonal patterns and the rhythms of nature, often engaging in ceremonial rituals to honor rain and the continued flow of life. Similarly, the Tarahumara people in Mexico have mastered the art of creating intricate systems of ditches and canals that lead to their fields, ensuring that every drop is used wisely. Such methods demonstrate a profound respect for the environment, encapsulating a holistic understanding that water is not merely a resource but a vital component of existence itself.

In stark contrast to these time-tested methodologies, contemporary challenges surrounding water conservation are intensifying. The ever-growing demand for freshwater because of population growth, industrialization, and agricultural expansion presents a formidable obstacle. Additionally, climate change exacerbates these issues, bringing unpredictable weather patterns, prolonged droughts, and severe flooding. Regions that once thrived with abundant water resources now scramble to adapt to decreasing supplies. Urban areas especially struggle, as infrastructure has often lagged behind the rapid expansion of populations, leading to overexploitation of aquifers. The implications of this scenario are dire; as access to clean water becomes increasingly scarce, social tensions rise, and the potential for conflict over these dwindling resources looms. Addressing these modern challenges will require innovative solutions that honor the age-old wisdom of indigenous practices while embracing new technologies and collaborative efforts to ensure sustainable water management.

Understanding both historical and contemporary water management practices reveals intertwined stories of human resilience and adaptability. Exploring these methods can inspire current and future generations to cultivate a deeper appreciation for water's value and integrate lessons from the past into modern strategies. To contribute to water conservation, one might consider simple everyday practices such as collecting rainwater for gardening or advocating for local sustainability initiatives. Every action counts, reminding us that harnessing the wisdom of our ancestors can lead us toward a more sustainable and equitable future.

12.3 Mythical Water Spirits and Their Cultural Significance

Water spirits hold a significant place in the mythology of numerous local tribes, representing the deep connection between culture and the vital element of water. These spirits are often perceived as guardians of rivers, lakes, and springs, embodying the essence of water and its life-giving properties. Stories of these entities are woven into the fabric of local traditions, where they are revered and sometimes feared. For instance, in many native tales, a water spirit may appear as a beautiful woman who beckons travelers close to the water's edge, only to reveal the dangers lurking beneath its surface. Such narratives not only enthrall listeners with their mystery but also serve to teach respect for water and its unpredictable nature. Through these narratives, tribes emphasize the importance of maintaining balance and harmony with the natural world, portraying water as both a precious resource and a powerful force. These mythical beings are integral to the cultural identity of local tribes, representing a profound understanding of their environment.

The influence of these myths extends well beyond storytelling, shaping cultural practices and instilling a sense of reverence for water resources that continues to this day. Rituals and ceremonies often involve offerings to water spirits, reinforcing the community's bond with the waterways that sustain them. For example, many tribes conduct seasonal rituals that honor the spirits and seek their blessings for bountiful harvests or safe journeys across waters. This practice is not simply about invoking supernatural favor; it highlights a traditional ecological knowledge that emphasizes harmony with water cycles and ecosystems. As modern challenges around water usage and conservation grow, these age-old beliefs provide a framework through which current

generations can approach environmental stewardship. The respect ingrained in these cultural practices serves as a reminder of the importance of water, encouraging sustainable interactions with this essential resource.

Travelers to places like the Grand Canyon can encounter remnants of these beliefs in modern-day practices and public art that reflect the local tribes' respect for water. Engaging with these cultures can lead to a deeper appreciation for the landscape and its historical significance, shedding light on the complexities of human interaction with nature. Understanding the role of water spirits in tribal folklore inspires a reflective approach to our own relationship with natural resources. It beckons each of us to recognize the stories behind the rivers and lakes we cherish, urging us to consider how we can honor and protect these sacred waters for future generations.

13. A Pathway to the Past: Trails and Routes

13.1 Ancient Trails: Pathways of the Ancients

T he ancient trails crisscrossing the Grand Canyon are not merely paths worn into the earth; they are the veins and arteries of an intricate cultural and trade network established by the indigenous peoples long before modern highways appeared. Each trail tells a story of movement, exchange, and connection, enabling tribes to share goods, traditions, and knowledge. The Havasupai, Hopi, and Navajo people utilized these routes to traverse the challenging terrain, transporting essential items like woven baskets and ceramic pottery, which represented not just commerce but also the very essence of their identities and livelihoods. The trails facilitated interactions that allowed for the sharing of resources and cultural practices that would shape the lives of generations. These pathways, shaded by ancient trees and rugged cliffs, served as lifelines, linking people to both nearby and distant communities forged by necessity and kinship.

As we walk these trails today, we connect with a past that echoes through time. Each step taken along these ancient pathways is an homage to the movements of the indigenous peoples who walked before us, tracing invisible threads of history across vast landscapes. The remnants of their journeys remind us of the deep-rooted connections that existed among the first inhabitants of this land, fostering unity and resilience in the face of adversity. Reflecting on these heritage trails opens a window into the rich tapestry of human existence, illustrating how geography influenced culture and how every footfall adds to our understanding of ancestral practices. They represent a larger narrative of human connection that transcends time, encouraging us to consider how our present is intertwined with the wisdom and traditions of those who came before.

To enrich your experience, consider taking a guided tour along these historic trails, where expert guides can share stories and insights about the indigenous cultures that thrived in this area. Pay attention to the surrounding landscape; every stone, every bend in the path holds the potential to reveal secrets of the ancients. Embracing this journey not only brings you closer to nature, but also deepens your appreciation for the vibrant history that pulses through the veins of the Grand Canyon.

13.2 Modern Trails: Hiking the Grand Canyon

The Grand Canyon is home to several major hiking trails, each offering its own unique adventure and breathtaking scenery. The Bright Angel Trail is one of the most popular routes, winding its way down into the canyon with well-maintained switchbacks, making it accessible for many hikers. This trail boasts water stations and rest areas, allowing for a more leisurely descent. As you trek along, you can experience the changing geology up close, from the rim's lush vegetation to the stark beauty of the canyon floor, where towering walls rise dramatically around you. In contrast, the South Kaibab Trail presents a more rugged experience. Without the amenities found on the Bright Angel Trail, it rewards those who trek its steep paths with jaw-dropping panoramic views. The early morning light casts an ethereal glow across the landscape, creating a fantastical, almost otherworldly atmosphere. Then there's the Hermit Trail, a lesser-known path that tends to attract fewer crowds. This trail is steep and challenging, but it leads to pristine wilderness areas, perfect for those seeking solitude amidst the canyon's grandeur. Each trail reveals different geological features and ecosystems, inviting hikers to connect deeply with this ancient landscape.

Trail etiquette is essential for preserving these natural pathways. By following some simple rules, everyone can enjoy the canyon's beauty while minimizing their impact on the environment. Always yield the trail to those ascending, as they usually have a more challenging climb and need the right of way. Keeping noise levels down not only respects fellow hikers but also allows for a more intimate experience with nature. Carrying out what you carry in is critical; this means no littering, as trash disrupts the natural charm and can harm wildlife. More importantly, staying on designated trails prevents erosion and protects the delicate flora and fauna that inhabit these ecosystems. Conservation efforts rely heavily on hikers taking responsibility for their surroundings. Respecting wildlife is also part of this etiquette. Observing animals from a distance and never feeding them ensures that they retain their natural behaviors, thereby preserving the delicate balance of their habitat.

Equipped with this understanding of the Grand Canyon's trails and the importance of preserving them, hikers can embark on their journeys with a sense of respect and responsibility. Choosing the right trail based on one's ability and the desired experience can enhance the adventure significantly. Before embarking on a hike, it's advisable to check for any trail conditions or advisories. Keeping hydrated and planning for the extremes of canyon weather will ensure a safe and enjoyable expedition into one of nature's most awe-inspiring wonders.

13.3 The Significance of Trails in Cultural Context

Trails hold deep cultural meaning in Indigenous traditions, representing both physical and metaphorical journeys. For many Indigenous peoples, a trail is more than a path led by footsteps; it is a historical narrative interwoven with the land, culture, and ancestral stories. Trails are used in various ceremonies, marking important routes traveled by ancestors, serving as conduits for sharing wisdom, and connecting generations. The act of traveling these paths often mirrors the spiritual journey one undertakes in life. They reflect personal growth and community ties, making them vital in teaching the youth about the significance of their heritage. The teachings imparted through these journeys are imbued with lessons of respect, stewardship, and a connection that transcends time and space, allowing individuals to engage with their history profoundly.

Moreover, trails symbolize connectivity not only among community members but also between the people and the land. They serve as physical reminders of shared experiences and collective struggles. Walking these paths can evoke memories of communal gatherings, trade, and ceremonies that have taken place over centuries. The land itself tells stories through trails, where each marker signifies a moment in time, a memory cherished and passed along. This connection fosters a sense of belonging and identity within Indigenous populations, intertwining their histories with the very earth they inhabit. Understanding this bond can enhance one's appreciation for the landscapes traversed, emphasizing the importance of protecting them. For anyone interested in exploring trails, engaging in these paths with an open heart and mind can reveal layers of history and connection that await beneath the surface.

When planning an adventure on these ancient trails, consider looking into local customs and stories surrounding them. Engaging with the local Indigenous communities can provide insights that enrich your experience. By honoring the significance of these routes, travelers can participate in a larger narrative—one that emphasizes respect, learning, and interconnectedness with history and nature. In seeking adventure, one does not merely follow a footpath; they tread on the stories of those who came before, leaving an imprint for those who will follow.

14. Indigenous Perspectives: Voices of the Land

14.1 The Role of Indigenous Knowledge in Environmental Stewardship

Indigenous perspectives offer a profound contribution to contemporary environmental practices and conservation efforts. These worldviews often emphasize a deep connection to the land, viewing nature not just as a resource to exploit but as a community to which humans belong. For many Indigenous people, every aspect of the environment is imbued with meaning, telling stories of creation and survival that have been transmitted through generations. This inherent understanding of ecological balance fosters sustainable practices that resonate with modern conservation goals. The intricate knowledge of local ecosystems, gained through centuries of observation and interaction, provides valuable insights into managing resources wisely. Practices such as controlled burns, seasonal harvesting, and restorative agriculture highlight how Indigenous strategies can address current environmental challenges like climate change and biodiversity loss.

In recent years, there have been successful collaborations between Indigenous communities and conservation organizations, showcasing the power of working together across cultural divides. These partnerships have often led to effective land management strategies that honor traditional knowledge while integrating scientific research. For instance, the collaboration with the Yurok Tribe in California focused on river restoration, aiming to revive salmon populations that are essential to both the ecosystem and Indigenous culture. Such efforts reveal the potential for blending ancient wisdom with contemporary science to create sustainable solutions. Other notable partnerships include the Inuit-led observatories in the Arctic, where Indigenous expertise is essential in monitoring climate changes. These collaborative frameworks not only enhance conservation efforts but also empower Indigenous communities, acknowledging their role as stewards of their ancestral lands.

Exploring the role of Indigenous knowledge in environmental stewardship provides not just a glimpse into the past but also a pathway forward. It challenges us to recognize the depth of understanding and practical wisdom embedded within these cultures. By valuing and integrating Indigenous perspectives in environmental action, society can move towards more holistic solutions. Engaging with local Indigenous communities, whether through travel or participation in conservation projects, presents an opportunity for deeper appreciation of their knowledge. This engagement not only benefits the environment but expands our own perspectives, encouraging a more sustainable and respectful relationship with the natural world.

14.2 Contemporary Indigenous Artists and Their Work

Contemporary Indigenous artists are increasingly drawing inspiration from the majestic landscapes of the Grand Canyon, creating powerful works that reflect their unique cultural heritage. The towering cliffs, vibrant colors, and diverse ecosystems of this natural wonder resonate deeply with artists who seek to express their connection to the environment. In this setting, the interplay of light and shadow, the shifting seasons, and the spirit of the land become integral to their creations. These artists often use traditional materials and techniques, merging them with modern influences to forge a new path in the art world. The Grand Canyon serves not only as a backdrop but also as a character in their narratives, embodying the stories, struggles, and victories of Indigenous peoples.

The art produced by these contemporary Indigenous creators carries rich themes that speak to tradition, identity, and the profound relationship with the natural world. Each piece reflects an intricate tapestry of cultural stories, symbolizing a deep reverence for ancestral knowledge and the land itself. For many artists, their work is a way to reclaim identity and tell the stories that may have been overshadowed by historical narratives. Whether through vibrant paintings, intricate sculptures, or mixed media installations, their art invites viewers to reflect on the cycles of nature, the significance of place, and the resilience of Indigenous cultures. The integration of natural materials, like earth pigments and fibers, emphasizes not only the beauty of the land but also the responsibility to protect and honor it.

Exploring this art can provide a deeper understanding of the complexities surrounding Indigenous identity today. It opens pathways to engage with the philosophies of many tribes that view land as a living entity, interconnected with personal and communal narratives. This connection challenges audiences to rethink their perspectives on history and heritage. When visiting the Grand Canyon, take the time to appreciate the art inspired by such a magnificent place and consider how it represents a bridge between the past and the contemporary world. Observing and discussing the intricate details of these artworks may enhance your appreciation for both the artist's message and the environment that shaped their vision.

14.3 Revitalizing Traditions: Cultural Resilience in the Face of Change

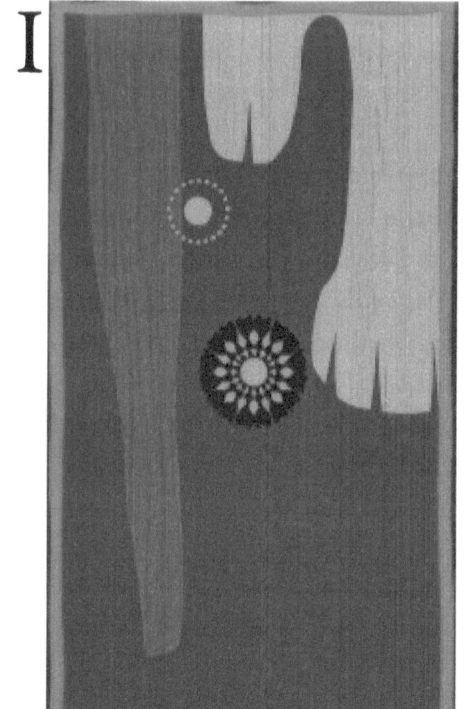

Indigenous communities across the globe are engaging in a remarkable resurgence of their cultural traditions, actively revitalizing practices that have faced the pressures of modernity. These communities are not just passively preserving what remains; they are innovating and adapting traditional arts, languages, and rituals to respond to contemporary issues. For instance, through the use of social media, younger generations disseminate stories and traditions, creating vibrant online spaces where culture thrives outside conventional boundaries. This active engagement helps bridge the gap between the ancient and the modern, allowing rich narratives and ancestral wisdom to influence not only Indigenous identity but also global conversations around sustainability and self-determination.

Cultural resilience plays a crucial role in the ability of these communities to maintain their identity and connection to the land. The deep ties to territory are rooted not just in history but in the very essence of who they are. When Indigenous peoples engage with their land through traditional practices, they are not merely recalling a past that is increasingly threatened; they are reinforcing their presence and continuity in the present. This connection is profoundly spiritual and practical, manifesting in ceremonies, stewardship of the land, and the passing down of ecological knowledge. Such actions affirm their rights to their ancestral territories, reinforcing a sense of belonging and purpose amidst modern challenges.

Embracing this cultural resilience does more than support identity; it ignites a spirit of adventure and exploration as communities seek to merge old practices with new realities. For travelers and adventurers, understanding these traditions offers a deeper experience of the landscapes they visit, such as the Grand Canyon, where history and modernity weave together. Engaging with local Indigenous guides can unveil hidden stories, invite reflection on the land's history, and reveal the significance of sacred sites. For anyone interested in archaeology or cultural studies, this interaction serves as a vivid reminder that history is not confined to ancient artifacts but is alive and evolving through the very people who inhabit these lands.

15. The Future of the Grand Canyon: Challenges and Opportunities

15.1 Navigating Tourism Growth: Strategies for Sustainable Travel

Promoting sustainable travel to the Grand Canyon involves a multifaceted approach that addresses the intricate balance between visitor enjoyment and environmental stewardship. One effective method is encouraging eco-friendly transportation options, such as shuttles and bike rentals, which reduce carbon emissions while allowing travelers to experience the beauty of the canyon in an intimate way. Partnerships with local Native American communities can also enhance sustainability by offering educational programs that emphasize historical and cultural significance, fostering a deeper understanding of the land's heritage. Furthermore, implementing visitor caps during peak seasons can alleviate overcrowding, preserving the natural beauty and serenity that many seek when visiting this unspoiled landscape. Enhanced visitor education programs about Leave No Trace principles can further instill a sense of responsibility, ensuring that the legacy of the Grand Canyon is preserved for future generations.

Several case studies illustrate successful strategies that balance visitor experiences with ecological preservation at the Grand Canyon. One notable example is the Grand Canyon Railway, which provides a scenic, green alternative to driving. This historic train journey allows visitors to enjoy the stunning landscapes while significantly lowering their carbon footprint. Another commendable initiative is the Grand Canyon Conservancy's efforts to restore degraded areas by engaging volunteers in reforestation and habitat restoration projects. These endeavors not only protect the ecosystem but also offer travelers a chance to contribute actively to conservation efforts. Additionally, adventure companies are pioneering guided eco-tours that educate participants on the unique geological formations and the indigenous cultures tied to the canyon, creating a fulfilling, enriching experience that resonates long after the journey ends.

In navigating sustainable travel, it is vital to recognize the impact each traveler has on this delicate environment. Exploring lesser-known trails or visiting during off-peak times can help mitigate overcrowding while allowing for a more personal adventure in this ancient wonderland. As you plan your journey, consider ways to support local initiatives and engage in practices that honor the land's culture and natural resources. Carry reusable water bottles, participate in local conservation efforts, and educate yourself about the profile of the ecosystems and communities you encounter. This conscious approach not only enhances the personal adventure but also contributes to the preservation of the Grand Canyon, enriching the experience for yourself and future explorers.

15.2 Engaging Local Communities in Preservation Efforts

Involving local communities in the preservation and stewardship of the Grand Canyon is essential for the sustainability of this natural wonder. Strategies that focus on building relationships with community members can create a sense of ownership, leading to a deeper commitment to conservation efforts. One effective approach is to establish partnerships with local organizations and indigenous groups, recognizing their knowledge and cultural ties to the land. Educational workshops and community meetings can foster dialogue, gathering insights on how best to protect the canyon's delicate ecosystems while honoring the rich histories of those who have lived in its shadows for generations.

Community engagement is not just beneficial for preservation; it also enhances sustainable tourism practices. When local residents are involved in tourism planning, they can ensure that it aligns with environmental conservation efforts and cultural integrity. For instance, involving local artisans in curating products and experiences can promote authentic representations of the area's heritage, while simultaneously generating income for these communities. This participatory model creates a circular economy that allows for the conservation of the Grand Canyon's natural beauty, ensuring that tourism enhances rather than undermines the local culture and environment.

By actively inviting locals to participate in the stewardship of the Grand Canyon, we embrace a future where tourism and community interests align harmoniously. To effectively engage with local communities, consider organizing events that allow visitors and residents to share stories, traditions, and visions for the future. These gatherings not only celebrate the canyon's wonder but also cultivate a shared understanding of the profound impact each visitor has on the preservation of this majestic landscape.

15.3 The Grand Canyon in the Age of Digital Exploration

Digital technology has transformed the way visitors experience the Grand Canyon. With the prevalence of smartphones and apps, explorers can access detailed maps, historical information, and interactive guides with just a few taps. This immediate access to knowledge enhances the connection between the physical space and the digital realm, allowing people to explore the canyon's vast beauty while learning about its geological formations and ancient cultures. Augmented reality experiences let visitors visualize life thousands of years ago, providing a powerful context that amplifies the awe of standing at the edge of the canyon. Moreover, social media platforms allow adventurers to share their experiences instantly, weaving personal narratives into the larger tapestry of the Grand Canyon's story and inviting others to partake in the journey.

Virtual tours and online resources elevate the understanding and appreciation of the Grand Canyon by making it accessible to those who may not be able to visit in person. High-definition videos transport viewers to the canyon's breathtaking vistas, while 3D simulations allow a sense of depth that flat images cannot convey. By exploring the stories behind the canyon's creation, its cultural significance to Native American tribes, and its role in natural history through virtual platforms, a wider audience can engage with its mysteries. Educational websites offer deep dives into the geological processes that shaped the canyon, creating a richer narrative that sparks curiosity. This virtual dimension not only provides a gateway for educational pursuits but also fosters a deeper emotional connection to the land, encouraging preservation and respect for this natural wonder.

Exploring the Grand Canyon digitally opens doors to a variety of experiences that tradition alone cannot provide. Embracing technology can enhance your journey, offering layers of understanding that redefine what it means to connect with the natural world. As you plan your visit, consider harnessing these digital tools. Download a guided audio tour before your trip or search for local wildlife webcams to catch glimpses of the canyon's inhabitants ahead of time. These resources can deepen your experience, guiding you not only through its physical trails but also through the rich tapestry of its history and culture.

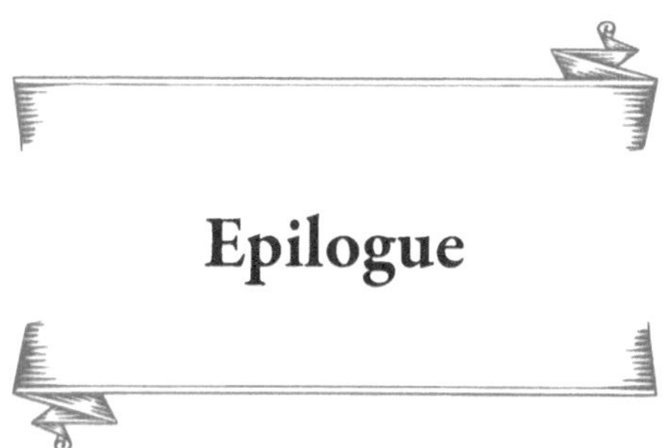

Epilogue

As we conclude our exploration of *Kincaid's Discovery: The Hidden Mysteries of the Grand Canyon*, one question looms large: what is it about these stories that captivate our imaginations, even in an era where information is just a click away? Whether truth or tale, the allure of a lost civilization hidden within the Grand Canyon represents something fundamental about our human spirit—a deep-seated fascination with the unknown and the possibility that mysteries lie just below the surface of our everyday lives.

Throughout this journey, we have traversed a landscape of exploration, curiosity, and speculation. From the tantalizing claims of G.E. Kincaid and the allure of ancient Egyptian artifacts to the playful hoaxes of Joe Mulhattan, each story reflects a powerful yearning—for discovery, for understanding, and for the wonder that comes with imagining worlds beyond our own. The Grand Canyon, with its majestic expanse and geological grandeur, serves as the perfect setting for these unfolding mysteries.

It's essential to recognize the cultural and historical climate that allowed such stories to flourish. In the late 19th and early 20th centuries, the world was enamored with archaeological expeditions and the rediscovery of ancient civilizations. Media outlets spun exciting narratives, often bending the truth for sensational headlines, while audiences delighted in tales of hidden treasures and forgotten races. Today, while we might approach such stories with skepticism, the core intrigue remains unchanged—do we too crave the mystery and magic these narratives offer?

What we take away from this exploration is not just the specifics of Kincaid's claims or the intricacies of Mulhattan's tall tales, but rather a celebration of the human imagination and the spirit of inquiry. In an age where information is abundant, the challenge lies in discerning fact from fiction while maintaining an open mind to the endless possibilities that stories like these present.

As you pause and gaze out at the Grand Canyon's vastness, remember that beneath its timeless beauty lie countless stories and secrets waiting to be uncovered. In the spirit of discovery, let us continue to explore, question, and marvel at the world's wonders—both above and below the surface.

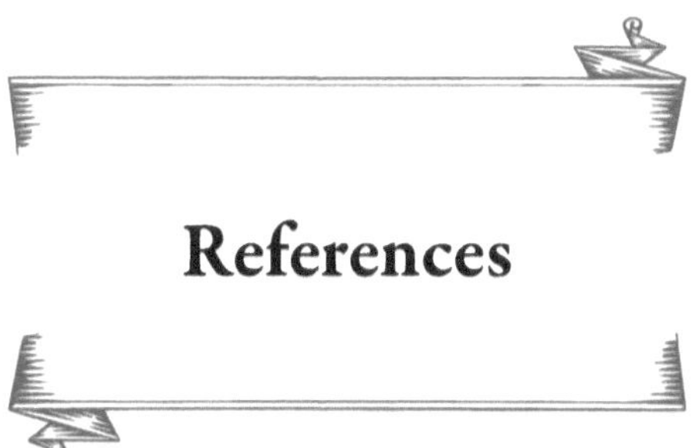

References

Arizona Gazette. "Exploration of Kincaid Cave." Arizona Gazette, April 5, 1909.

Smith, John D. Mysteries of the Grand Canyon: Legends and Discoveries. New York: Canyon Press, 2018.

Johnson, Emily. "Theories on Kincaid's Cave: Archaeological Perspectives." Journal of Southwestern Archaeology 22, no. 3 (2020): 312-329.

Carter, Thomas R. Ancient Echoes: Native American Legends of the Grand Canyon. Tucson: Desert Trails Publishing, 2019.

Miller, Susan L. Beyond the Horizon: A History of Exploration in the American West. Denver: Western Historical Press, 2021.

Smithsonian Institution Archives. "Correspondence on Archaeological Expeditions, 1908-1910." Washington, D.C.: Smithsonian Institution.

Jones, Kevin. "Evaluating the Kincaid Cave Narrative: Hoax or Hidden Treasure?" History and Mythology Quarterly 15, no. 2 (2021): 156-178.

Tucker, Michael. "Into the Canyon: Modern Day Explorations and Discoveries." Podcast episode, Exploration Chronicles. August 14, 2023.

Brown, Lisa M. Protectors of the Sacred: Indigenous Perspectives on the Grand Canyon. Flagstaff: Northern Arizona University Press, 2022.

NATIONAL PARK SERVICE. "Grand Canyon Geology and Archaeology." Accessed March 1, 2024. https://www.nps.gov/grca/learn/nature/geology.htm.

About the Author

Cassiel E. Nox is a renowned writer whose works transcend the boundaries of science, mystery, and imagination. Known for developing intricate tales, these stories merge conspiracy theories, metaphysics, and the latest discoveries in quantum physics. The science fiction narratives are both captivating and thought-provoking. With a passion for exploring the hidden mysteries of the universe, the writing delves deep into subjects such as extraterrestrial life, ancient secret knowledge, and cryptic phenomena. Cassiel's storytelling prowess is apparent in "Hidden Depths: The Kincaid Conspiracy and The Secrets of The Grand Canyon" and "Beyond The Collider: CERN's Quantum Rift And The Mandela Effect Mystery." In these stories, the intersections of scientific experiments and anomalous collective memories, often called the Mandela Effect, are not just brought to life, but they captivate the reader, holding their attention from start to finish. The journey continues with "From Roswell to Today: The Timeline of UFOs and Aliens," an exciting exploration of historical and contemporary accounts of UFO sightings and extraterrestrial phenomena. Cassiel is working on a science-fiction series called "When Something is Nothing," which promises to expand the horizons of imagination and intrigue further. Venturing into the world of science fiction, Cassiel crafts narratives that transport readers to distant stars and futuristic societies, all while grounded in scientific plausibility and human experience. With a background steeped in academic research and a passion for unraveling conspiracies, Cassiel E. Nox remains a distinctive voice in speculative fiction, inviting audiences to question the boundaries of reality and dream beyond the known.

Read more at https://my.ionos.com/domain-details/ quantumwriterverse.com.